Contents

Anna Jackson
Foreword — vii

Ben Kemp
The Monks Who Tend the Garden with Tiny Scissors

    Juni-Gatsu — 3
    Food to Song
        1. ご飯 Rice — 5
        2. Kūmara — 6
        3. お茶 Green Tea — 7
        4. Kūkupa — 8
    Opoutere — 9
    Oto — 11
    Four Tokyo Subcultures — 12
    The Japanese Moko — 15
    Ranginui's Tomb — 16
    Two Vignettes of a Warrior
        Part 1: Miyamoto — 18
        Part 2: Te Kooti — 19
    The Walker Flower and the Potiki Tree — 20
    The Essence of I — 21

Vanessa Crofskey
Shopping List of Small Violences

Postcard from Rainbow's End	29
I used to play the silent game even during lunch breaks	30
Remuera	32
dumplings are fake	33
New Zealand Passenger Arrival Card	35
ptsd memes for the anxious / avoidant teen	36
There's Real Mānuka Honey in Heaven	40
Foyer Fucking	41
beauty	44
Guide Notes	45
Recipe for a Funeral	46
(🤢)	49
Shopping List of Small Violences	50
Chart Title	51
Glory Be to Family Planning	54
Ex-Partners Have Called Me a Baptism	56
two-piece bathing suits	57
+ / −	60
The Capital of My Mother	61
To All the Boys I've Loved Before	64

AUP new poets 6

Ben Kemp
Vanessa Crofskey
Chris Stewart

Edited and with a foreword
by Anna Jackson

AUCKLAND
UNIVERSITY
PRESS

Chris Stewart
Gravity

navigator	69
gravity	70
everyone wants to know how heavy they are	71
embers	72
flecks of ice	73
mummy	74
you have too many dreams to be asleep	75
a tooth emerges	76
you take a tunnel to the sea	77
time's handle locks from the inside	78
I have no juice for you to suck	79
profit	80
there are no angels but the children of mice and eagles	81
male seahorses bear the young	82
scarf	83
rusty bones	84
inflammation	85
Russian dolls	86
your father was also buried	87
frost	88
my father the elephant	89
The history of his bridge	90
the chef	91
Like stone flowers a dead man	92

Notes   95

Foreword

AUP New Poets 6 presents three very different poets, Ben Kemp, Vanessa Crofskey and Chris Stewart, who each offer a distinctive approach in terms of both form and content. We move from Ben Kemp's slow-paced attentive readings of place and people, in a selection moving between Japan and New Zealand, to the velocity of Vanessa Crofskey's fierce, funny, intimate and political poetry, which takes the form of shopping lists, Post-it notes, graphs, erasures, a passenger arrival card and even *poetry*, and finally to Chris Stewart's visceral take on the domestic, the nights cut to pieces by teething, the gravity of love and the churn of time. Yet there are common strands too, as these poets all perform their own acts of archaeology, unearthing bones, uncovering secrets, finding solace and significance in food, testing cultural change and difference, drawing connections between people and finding in other people everything that is needed: as Vanessa Crofskey writes, 'if I don't have wifi then I do have a cell phone to ask my mother how cold it is in another city'.

> Walking to work,
>   a stone wall shoulders my path . . .
>   it was built 700 years ago
>   by monks who tended the gardens with
>   tiny scissors &   a clear mind

These beautifully paced lines from Ben Kemp's 'Juni-Gatsu' introduce an aesthetic that runs through all his poetry, a way of moving through the world attentive to detail and to the constant, the still and the historical, valuing clarity and the neatly tended. This aesthetic shapes the look of his poetry on the page, the beautiful stanza shapes and spacious unfolding of lines and sentences, and can be seen too in the careful choice of words, the stone wall that 'shoulders' the poet's path and, later in the poem, a 'fragile' frost, people 'the temperament of porcelain'.

Born in Gisborne in 1972 and brought up in Manutuke and Matawhero, of Rongowhakaata roots, Kemp first travelled to Japan at the age of twenty-three, and returned to Tokyo in 2002. A musician and songwriter, Kemp played on the street in Shimo Kitazawa, one of the more Bohemian areas of Tokyo well known for its vibrant music scene and, with musician Koyu Suzuki, was soon performing at some of Tokyo's most prestigious live venues. Throughout the poems in Kemp's selection for this volume, we find him with 'ears attuned to performers entranced within tunnels, / their folded legs, / affront music aficionados baptised in coffee and single malt whisky', but with ears attuned too to quieter sounds, hearing wind through the grass as 'the song of a 10,000-piece orchestra with no sheet music or conductor' or 'listening with ears to the thin walls of the sky, / like *shōji* doors that pierce when the planes scatter like needles through silk'.

Setting kūmara alongside white rice, wood pigeon alongside green tea, Kemp writes as a New Zealander even in poems located in Japan. In 'The Japanese Moko', the bone chisel is 'at rest beside an earthen teapot', and 'the wrinkled shadow of this warrior, with one *wabi-sabi* eye' is found 'in kūmara garden / and under night's sky'. In 'Ranginui's Tomb', Ranginui can be found 'wandering through the / narrow streets of Gōtoku-ji', holding 'the wounded sky in his hand'. These poems move between Japan and New Zealand, observation and memory, the contemporary and the historical, the personal and the imaginary, a cuckoo singing in 1584 and beings flaunting LCD eyes 'with hardwired electricity cables to their temples'. The precision of the details in these poems is matched by the scope of the empathy and imagination Kemp shows as he looks through the eyes of a stranded whale, seeing the world for the first time 'without the lens of seawater', and presents his own Whitman-like self as made up of all those people he has passed by in his travels, along with the landscapes he has loved on his journey to the sea.

Vanessa Crofskey begins her selection with a poem about her dislike of talking: 'I would public protest with black tape, bound wrists and a righteous vow of silence just to avoid it'. Swimming offers a brilliant way to avoid smalltalk, and the uncanny observation she makes that a scream screamed underwater is converted into 'laughter bubbled into / pearled pops and gargled sound bites' offers an unnerving way of understanding the humour that makes her poetry so much fun to read and share. Just as the poems themselves take many different forms, they also chronicle the many forms communication can take – postcards, screenshots, the comments section of a recipe site, a 'civil conversation' in a cafe when things are pretty much over, 'fights like filmic mosquito bites', phone calls, emojis, 'curt emails about when an appropriate time to Skype would be'.

A graduate of Auckland University of Technology with a BVA in sculpture, Basement Theatre producer in residence in 2018, currently working as a staff writer for *The Pantograph Punch* and as a curator at the University of Auckland Window Gallery, Crofskey brings a multidisciplinary approach to poetry. While the visual and design elements are immediately striking on the page, she comes to poetry through spoken word, and the power of her work in performance has seen her receive a number of slam poetry awards including the Best Spoken Word award at the Auckland Fringe festival in 2017 and the 2017 Auckland Regional Slam Championship. Amanda Robinson's description of the effect of a Vanessa Crofskey performance is true to my experience too: 'Between poems she's sarcastic and self-deprecating, but when she begins a poem she silences the room, save for a synchronised sharp exhale when she drops a line like "Weren't you an open casket for the reckless?" She is in total control of her intonation; even her breaths feel calculated.'

That self-deprecation of course is present in many of the poems too, but it is a complex self-deprecation, at once funny, poignant, vulnerable, controlled and aware of the social and political context which both accounts for this need to put herself down, and in which she uses self-deprecation to make subtle and powerful points. Body image, romantic entanglements, pop culture, anxiety, disassociation, ideas of beauty and ethnic stereotyping all come into play as competing tensions and colliding possibilities.

Of Hokkien Chinese and Pākehā descent, Crofskey writes of being 'so authentic i use chopsticks to eat macaroni'. Identity is complicated, and some of the ways in which it is constructed in contemporary society are really funny. But thinking about identity can be serious emotional work too, as a powerful poem like 'The Capital of My Mother' demonstrates, exploring the complex mixture of heredity, kinship ties, cultural difference, displacement and time that extended family involves. 'I cannot find home except the sense / of somewhere I can't reach', she writes, 'I am a migrant's remembrance / I am a welcome party'.

'Time's handle locks from the inside', reads the title of one of Chris Stewart's poems – he has a talent for titles. For all the visionary imagination that takes these poems into such strange territory, as facts and observations take off into metaphor and simile, and into dream and the surreal, there is a hard-won realism to these poems. A secondary school English teacher, Stewart took a year of part-time teaching to look after his two pre-school daughters, and writes powerfully about the demands of parenting small children. Parenthood opens up vast reservoirs of love – in 'inflammation' the father taking up his desperate vigil over the child in the hospital's respiration room, wishes he could tunnel into the child's lungs to defeat the enemy he hears as bees – but it also involves sacrifice, incarceration and a transformation of the self that can never be undone. After bathing a small daughter by firelight, he wonders 'perhaps my forehead stretch-marked / as my frontal lobe grew / a new fold'. As parenthood stretches into the future, time takes on a new urgency and depth, transforming, too, memories of the poet's own childhood and his relation to his own parents.

Parenthood is physical, instinctive and natural – but nature has all kinds of patterns for parenthood, from the penguin father who sits on the egg while the mother hunts fish, to the scorpion wary of his daughter's sting. Nature can't always be turned to for answers – 'I went to the panda she told me / to leave one daughter behind / I went to the mouse he told me / to eat both my daughters / I went to the worm it told me / to let my daughters eat me' – yet the animal imagery that runs all through this collection does offer surprising moments of recognition, as does the imagery of space travel, alchemy, archaeology, mining and the Gothic (the father as Egyptian mummy). Several of these poems draw on the particular derangement that comes with the sleep deprivation of early parenthood, and it is not only in the poems directly about teething that we find tooth imagery working its way in. One poem ends with the bleak statement 'in a year of sleep you never complete / a dream'. Yet perhaps these poems are a form of dream completion, as the wild inventiveness, strange resonance and desperate emotions usually confined to dreaming find their way, through these poems, into the light.

The image from Ben Kemp's 'Juni-Gatsu' of the carp rising to the light resonates for me with the work poetry does:

> the carp bask under muddy glass …
>   sometimes twelve or thirteen at a time,
>   trading their safety for the sun …

All three of these poets write beyond safety, writing about difficult and painful subjects as well as things they value both big and small. *AUP New Poets 6* includes poems about whale strandings, teething, dispossession, loss, the pain of physical exercise, the embarrassment of swimwear, the gravity of responsibility; as well as poems about clean sheets, rice, bathing a child, white-washed pages, red ink, the love you feel with the shiver of your skin, friends to watch *Ferris Bueller's Day Off* with, parents to the rescue, cherry blossom and the chatter of 10,000 seagulls.

Anna Jackson

Ben Kemp

The Monks Who Tend the Garden with Tiny Scissors

Juni-Gatsu
(December)

Japan is delicate,
& in December when snow settles upon the branches,
    it feels like a Buddhist prayer ...

Walking to work,
a stone wall shoulders my path ...
    it was built 700 years ago
        by monks who tended the gardens with
            tiny scissors &   a clear mind

Walking to work,
my fingertips hang out from under the sleeves of my jacket ...
    tickled by a morning sun & a frost,   fragile,
    like the ribs of a leaf ...

Walking to work,
the peddlers in steaming noodle carts have faces like nourished hide ...

    if you get close,
    their foreheads are old photos,
        with grandfathers, mothers,
            brothers & uncles,   resting over their brow

walking to work from Yoyogi-Uehara, where I live ...
    it's saintly ...

    when the sun hits the orange tile roofs
    knelt down through the night ...
        they rise to their feet.

& in Shinjuku, where I work, the people the temperament of porcelain,
    with cheekbones
    like Zen ...
        & Kurosawa

& in the canal,
        the carp bask under muddy glass ...
                sometimes twelve or thirteen at a time,
                trading their safety for the sun,

& over the bridge with wide hips & feet resting in a puddle ...

I enter the arteries of Tokyo ...
        with ears open ...

listening for you
        for Manutuke
                the Te Arai ...
                      & the sound of oranges growing.

Food to Song

1. ご飯 *Rice*

Rice,

White moonlight,
with an undershirt of calcium,
held aloft in two wooden fingertips
the trail of seeds to Jōmon.

Old people,
koshihikari, the taste of the *shakuhachi*,
a singular stream of air,
with toes in white waterways of phosphorus.

Dusty bones,
draped in a cloth of translucent starch,
a pearl in soma,
swell the iron rich children of grass.

Copper pot,
under the pirouette of watery ghosts,
in a cot over white ash,
the lively chatter of 10,000 seagulls.

A shed husk,
scented of one grain,
this white cloak was a shelter
to one universe that withheld the map to god.

2. Kūmara

Sweet potato,

Taputini,
a voyage to Polynesia east,
an offering of kūmara
brings tears to the eyes of Toroa.

Matariki,
behold the eyes of god,
clear and bright this constellation of stars,
a pathway of light to harvest.

Hutihuti,
the blessings of Rongo-mā-Tāne
rest at the toes of spring,
tapu mounds of soil scatter the hillsides.

Rekamaroa,
a bed of hot riverstones,
under the earthen blanket,
steam rises, the buttery smell of pork belly.

Houhere,
creamy fingers to open mouth,
mīere, mīere, oh mīere
upon a honeyed tongue, spirited tīpuna sing.

3. お茶 *Green Tea*

Green tea,

A leaf,
susurrates amid the voices of millions,
the soul of Zen priest Eisai
in an ancient garden of luminous green sunlight.

A teahouse,
under branches, the antiquated maple,
a square box with wooden bones,
shōji eyes and *tatami* feet.

Jyaku, wa, sei, kei,
tranquility, in green shadows
harmony, quintessence of the tea flower
from *chawan* to lip, purity and respect.

Suffuse manganese
with supple verve, a warrior
his serene shoulders, *shōkyaku*
observes the halcyon view of his inner self.

Emperor Saga,
the path to Bonshakuji temple,
with bamboo growing perpendicular to the sky,
a legacy of *macha*, swaddled in steam.

4. *Kūkupa*

The wood pigeon,

Bush floor,
spindles, green then gold sunlight,
water tinkles over rocks,
in feathered cloak, Rupe descends the underworld.

In treetops,
Tāranga's white apron,
iridescent copper and green wings,
roosting, in the wooded forearms of Tāne-mahuta.

At sunrise,
Haumia-tiketike's hands,
with nectar and wild berries,
her bounty, sweetening the flesh of the kūkupa.

The hunter,
with snares tied to the karaka branches,
pours water into a trough.
The flax noose awaits a fattened neck to break.

Umu stone,
hoven in supple mauri arms,
riverbed to under earth, as steam rises,
awaiting the warm oils of flesh to Aunty Heni's lip.

Opoutere
(Whale stranding)

The sound of a piano is ringing through this ocean,
four simple notes alongside,
tied together by the fisherman's knot,
with the ends neatly clipped.

The tide is low, shallow in this sink,
the shoulder of the coast is no longer submerged,
my belly rested on the seabed.
I have not the strength to ask, but I am listening ...

The piece of music is biological,
an algorithm with an end,
four primary colours on a palette that is the arm of the painter.
I am your brush ...

The bed upon which my belly rests is warm,
finer than feathers ...
A casket around my body, but no dark hole ...
Opoutere.

Gentle hands and a rocking chair,
      and from their palms the same four notes,
      but not a piano ...
      a gut-string guitar ...
      handed down through four generations,
infant, girl, woman and grandmother.

The branches of my whakapapa are being clipped
with secateurs,
and musical instruments, unfretted.
My carcass is made up of leaves that fall in spring ...
Opoutere.

How far have I travelled?
The miles have collapsed but the seawater is made up of tukutuku panels,
Navigating our way through the whare,
I am inside ...

She is wailing, weaving freshly picked flax between the four notes,
My ears tell me she is beautiful ...
For there is no seam in her voice ...
I drink ...   but my vessel is almost dry.

We are one tree, one body ...
fed by the same root and connected by the same fisherman's knot,
I am my brothers and sisters and they are me ...
Opoutere.

My skin is growing cold, dry,
spilling a glass of clear oil that is swallowed up by the sand.
        The oil is the mystery of consciousness,
            an undefined quantity that now runs through their fingers.
I did not ask, but I am grateful for their help ...

I have never seen without the lens of seawater,
the undulation of the ocean is like a pulse.
I have fallen ...   but the music has not died for the instrument is now a
        bamboo flute,
                and a child ...

My mother is near me but she is dead now,
dissolving into the tukutuku panels.

Gentle hands and the rocking chair, carved from the finest tree,
Crafted by the most gifted of makers ...

I did not ask ...   and you came ...
Opoutere.

Oto
(Sound)

As the cherry blossom falls in acid rain
                  my eye bursts into sketches of
                                red ink and
                                bamboo
and Meiji Jingū,
                        with white-washed pages and a delicate spine,
                        like a leaf in one's fingertips under a sun

Our knuckles were white in 1945
                flipping glances,
                      and leaving behind a whole generation
          of stark, wrinkled branches
                      and solace ...   my love ...

For only after 8am and before 3pm,   will I pray
                            like buckled bridges
                            and twisted metal ...

                                      silent for now but still breathing
                feathers tickling their swirling lips,
                with a twist of sea eggs.

Four Tokyo Subcultures

In Shimokitazawa, these sinewy alleyways
      among the echoes of Kerouac
and the grungy fingertips of Orwell

stride piano rings through humid
      late night summer streets,
collide with the 12-string jangle of a candy red Rickenbacker,

textured buildings both old and new,
running my fingers over the DNA of a neighbourhood with
      crooked theatres, hand-hewn bookshops,
broken clothes hanging on fences and the wonderful waft of the evaporating
      oils of *okonomiyaki*,

ears attuned to performers entranced within tunnels,
      their folded legs,
affront music aficionados baptised in coffee and single malt whisky
the deadly kiss of creepy record labels.

Shimokitazawa
of meticulous inelegance and stylised disorganisation tucked into those
      glorious nooks and crannies.

∞

In Kabukicho, under a black blanket
colourful lights bulge as vertical waterfalls,
      the embroidery of sleaze to
grind the senses to dust.

The infinite sea of gauche salarymen,
      unzipping and zipping their flies,
a mould for intimacy replicated a million times

with oranged-out faces,
the hosts huddle on street corners in cheap suits
    with convoluted hairstyles
and fragmented dispositions that bark Zen.

'The bad hand'
    yakuza concealed in lightless pockets,
step out towards beautiful girls
    in tatty kimonos,
wooing their cash cows from pasture to plate.

'Soap-land'
    the alchemy of the handjob from detestation
to the inner chamber of purity.

∞

In Asakusa, you run the back of your hand along
    the frayed seam of Tokyo old
Sensō-ji temple of dissipated shadows
    where samurai squint at the distended vista
of modernisation and extinction.

Haru,
in early evening, a flock of red lanterns
    flicker, flutter in sultry air
while over stonewalls, the *Nohkan* flute is the breeze
    and inside those walls
under cherry blossom trees
    of pink, pink
the casting of ancient candlelight onto Noh masks,
revitalising the embers of old stories.

Shitamachi is 'the low city'
of good fortune, enlightenment of the lotus flower

of indefinite wishes, posted near Kaminarimon gate
with buildings gracefully worn
as the aged taper off.

∞

Akihabara, where electricity flows in arteries
        amid shimmering arcades
and neon signs so dizzy with the transfiguration
of the Japanese soul,

of altered dimensions, where fanboys and fangirls
        crawl into 2D pages
with smudged handprints on the inside of comics,
the anime and manga portent
        morphed into religious precepts
to define *otaku*.

Chūō-dōri street is wide with outstretched arms to the blue sky
        coughing incessantly above
the intricate tributaries that run off into pools
        of eccentric collectors.

Beings flaunt LCD eyes
with hardwired electricity cables to their temples,
        no sunlight.

In 'Akiba' town,
incandescent lights collide with the otherness of cosplay,
        these multitudes crusading to perfect
their electronic god.

The Japanese Moko

The ridge over his nose
yields a trickle of blood,
the bone chisel at rest beside an earthen teapot.

In kūmara garden,
and under night's sky,
the wrinkled shadow of this warrior, with one *wabi-sabi* eye.

Crows,
feathered in melanin,
and contoured by rivers of ink that cascade to a clay floor.

A journey,
dirt track by horseback,
in rice fields of Tūmatauenga,
the Kami-sama with a muscle to plough.

Rangatira drinks,
in a valley of flax and green tea,
this hewed vignette, as the manifesto to his curved soul.

Ranginui's Tomb

1. Ranginui broke down into pieces,
wandering through the
narrow streets of Gōtoku-ji,
he held the wounded sky in his hand,
muttering words of no language . . .
autumn, winter, summer, spring had no shape bundled together like knotted
string within his closed fist.

2. His feet upon the abdomen of Papatūānuku,
laying warm fingers upon stiff flesh,
'She never felt like this' locked in his volts of bracken and seawater . . .
'They never bothered to look under their feet, did they?'

3. Through scattered crowds of priests, carpenters, factory workers and
rusted cans, he squeezed the seasons in his hand,
then laid them out on the tar seal and tried to unravel them,
his brow as heavy as concrete,
concrete laid by the construction workers passing by,
precise dots and long canals of steel they built, without memory.

4. The crowds parted for him,
like Moses without his God, he would have drowned,
Ranginui was no Māori god, not then . . .
A beggar and a paper cup, looking for the ends of the string he'd lost,
four seasons, eight ends and toxic clouds.

5. Ranginui was the name given to him by his father,
behind the shroud of the sky . . .
listening with ears to the thin walls of the sky,
like *shōji* doors that pierce when the planes scatter like needles through silk.

6. Ranginui was never a boy,
the weight of the sky would have been too great for growing shoulders,
so he was conceived with limbs like a tōtara tree, his eyes unfolding the
colours like origami as they entered, passing through the gate.

7. The same fingers that now fumbled through the dirty string,
eroded like riverstones on the curbs of the bank.

8. The woman at the butcher's shop perished at the sight of Ranginui's despair,
she fell through the cracks of the street,
into the hole that opened up for her when she realised her sky father had fallen like a pigeon.

9. When she looked up, the sky was not there,
of constructs and bones,
the decorative silks pulled down to the earth,
like tugging the cloth from the kitchen table.

10. Ranginui lay his body over the string of that he could not untangle,
his arms outstretched, his left cheek flush to the white line, his feet foraging for cover like a crab in the sand,
he held tight to the midrib of Papatūānuku digging his fingers into the curve of her lower back,
and there he stayed.

11. No one ever noticed him and never did they realise the sky was empty,
the clothes torn down,
only the beams and naked nails above that weaken little by little,
until finally they will fall,
the branches will split at the trunk of the tree ...

12. The tree that grows in someone else's garden.

Two Vignettes of a Warrior

Part 1: Miyamoto

Suffuse the scent of a peach blossom
amid red pines.
In 1584, Banshu,
a cuckoo sings Bennosuke

A baby with irritable skin
builds the tall man,
a vision of two swords, Niten Ichi
'two heavens as one'

The dead follow Sasaki,
blinded by sunlight,
the last swish of a wooden sword, *bokken*
that severs the swallow's tail

Of Zen,
no blue, no sky,
unravelling subjective layers of experience,
and dissolve into emptiness

Cave Reigandō, 1645,
squints an eye,
then rises to tighten his belt,
in his left hand, *katana*,
with one knee raised vertically to heaven.

Part 2: Te Kooti

A vision in 1830,
of one death, one birth,
a dark reflection in Awapuni lagoon, Te Toiroa
Rikirangi, the horse trader and sailor

Coastal rain,
a raged eye and taut lip,
chin to the bush pigeon, Urewera
his scrub beard asleep in the undergrowth

Inside the arc
the immaculate heads of women and children,
utu, swings the tomahawk
so softly spoken 'ko ana ki te poti!'

Upraised hand
bade unto God, Ringatū
the Israelites' phosphorus flame,
a Hauhau disciple to hāngī at Jacob's table

'Pinepine te kura', 1893,
in shade beneath an unyielding sun,
the last psalm, the last waiata,
the tooth of injustice is blunt, the prophet extinguished.

The Walker Flower and the Potiki Tree
(To Brian Potiki and Jill Walker)

Northeast,
abridges the kōkako song
and the incense of smoking trout

Be blue,
in the chest of the lake,
the sway of oxygen weed
and the shimmer of his nylon strings

A tree, a flower
to flourish in a flown nest,
amongst the tickle of butterflies
and the swish of the fish's tail

The tarsal moulded in clay,
under filaments and ferns
a song, her voice
to lift the spirit
and sweeten the apples growing in their garden.

The Essence of I
(Ode to Walt Whitman)

Salt my song …
In the shallow of a valley that would come to pass,
with the smell of the faraway coast lifting my nostrils to the horizon,
travelling birds
… I am no longer here.

The clouds, the milk of my young eyes
at the table chewing gum
fostering my backyard of mental junk
the soul, and loose bicycle chains,
the rubber tyres and inner tubes, endless loops of thinking.

I saw a man, a farmer carved from marble,
his hands shaped so fine,
through mud and an eel-laden stream he stepped,
carrying the hardware of his engine,
blinking eyes, like a tap running and a verse undivided, yet to be sung.

The fences, penning boundaries and clenching teeth to
warn off the others,
'others' their memories strapped to their backs,
onward into the deeper valley,
their noses to the clouds, scenting the waves and the redemption of the sea.

Perched on the fence post, where it plateaued,
like the forehead of the hill lying down,
I imagined, then I saw an owl in daylight,
I shuddered …

On the opposite slope the winds ripped through,
picking up loose hitchhikers and skidding through grass tops,
I heard the song of a 10,000-piece orchestra with no sheet music or conductor,
with molecules for instruments and voices.

Salt of my song ...
I centred myself, approximately in the middle of the paddock,
opened my mouth and expunged my lungs of all anxiety,
the grass momentarily engulfed me, then receded to tickle my feet,
the mud giggling through my toes.

I asked for the reasons of hardship, for me and my brother and sisters,
the river running a steady pulse, 200 yards from the origin of my inquiry.
The river rose from its back and the sky stepped down from its ladder.
They shuffled in on either side of me and placed their fingertips upon
the temples of my head, one finger on either side.
      I wept at the depth of their love, and they smiled.

At the edge of the property was an old abandoned shack,
the wood eaten by age,
but within was a palace adorned with every jewel and known mastery of
      craftsmanship,
I travelled to the edge of the farm, 34 years it took me to arrive,
forever departing, departing, day after day ...
On my arrival I was welcomed with acute silence,
an unprecedented celebration with no band, people or sentiment,
just clarity ...

Salt of my song ...
How would the sea look? Dressed in cloaks and fine jewellery,
pinstriped red trousers and yellowed diamonds hanging from its limbs.
I'm not sure if the creatures within would stand for it,
mocking and murmuring for the old clothes to be worn again,
'bring the ancestors back!' they would shout I'm sure,
... blue-nothing she wore.

At the west side, where winter is,
the snow is translucent and sweet to taste.
I journeyed there at the age of 11 and found the nicest old man and a little old
      woman,

bent over backwards like the 'U' at the bottom of a drainpipe.
They were carrying snow from one side of the field to the other,
smoothing out the creases, ensuring the brightness and air within remained.
I understand the purpose of their work.
'Purpose' is just one grain of sand … surrender,

the river is so beautiful,
embroidered with willow trees and intricately shaped banks, like pottery,
the craftsman gently pressing fingers into the side, just above the hipbone,
     the water, each atom with knapsack slung over shoulder,
filled with books and millions of songs, poems and anecdotes of wisdom.
I wish I could step inside and press shoulders.
I am waiting to be a river.

I yearn sometimes …
I am drawn, stretched out like leather over a drum,
trying to remove my feet from this soil.
The clouds overhead like canopies of gloom, and real restriction,
there is no tributary to carry me,
no rootstock or trunk to feed the leaves, and my branches,
whispering below the decibels, where purity is not here or there,
but 'nothingness in me, brother'.

Underground are the ancestors lined up in single file,
feathers in their hair, with paintbrushes for fingers and flutes for mouths.
In the darkness that is their light they are whole,
yet the line they form is for me,
carrying the burden of my impatience, they vent it.
I often pierce my hands through the earth, arms dug deep,
softer in the tractor tracks, we touch hands.
The movements in hand, saying we love each other …

The northeastern tip is the desert,
I hitched a ride on that wind-blowing orchestra,
and I found a well,

       my consciousness, and perfect white sunlight on a vast bed of sand . . .
The well was filled with embers, breathing smoke,
I sat for days contemplating its meaning to me,
these loose and odd snippets.
Why burn? Why burn?

Covering the entire property, just one inch from its surface is a clear film
       unseen to the eye.
I have speculated its presence.
For a matter of seconds only when light and darkness are side by side,
elongated shadows and settling birds,
I have glimpsed it, peering backstage through the burgundy curtain,
The seam and the supporting beam of . . .

And who have I passed on my travels?
A teacher,
a man thrashing himself with guilt,
one soul who pulled entire landscapes from his lips, and the darkness
       between,
a businessman and a blond schoolboy,
a traveller with thirteen typewriters, three working and the rest . . . well just
       sentimentality really,
a sportsperson pushing his walls out,
an aging young man who sat me down, plastered me with words, labels and
       posters,
then left,
a baby,
a clerk with every instrument of art strapped to his body,
a walking shell,
and someone, like a ghost that I have never seen but always felt.

Salt my song . . .
I have to love you,
and this farmland upon which I live.
I evolve here.

One day I will journey to the sea,
become that river and dissolve into the essence of I.

Vanessa Crofskey

Shopping List of Small Violences

Postcard from Rainbow's End

I wish I was heartbroken at the top of Mt Fuji
or in deep plunging overdraft in the rouged canyons of Germany
or so depressed I can't speak but in Disneyland, California
or maybe just sad on a nice black-sand beach

I don't believe in pathetic fallacy as a metaphor for anything
It can't Tiger Balm my heart for proven pain relief
My blisters still peel like mandarins and I still
graze my hands on gravelled conversations

I thought if we only communicated in postcards

I thought if we only communicated via boring methods
like curt emails about when an appropriate time to Skype would be

I'm emotionally
attracted to unavailable men in damp hotels
whose unsent texts never lose their lustre

I'd rather feel like shit in luxury
than pick a fight with Alison Bechdel, or
the next guy on Tinder wearing a stupid band shirt I've never fucking listened to

Even if he has a dad bod
Even if his mum's house has central heating

Anyhow, if you want me,

I'll be nursing margaritas at a day spa in Bali
picking at my French harp which sounds excruciatingly lovely

I used to play the silent game even during lunch breaks

The consequences of silence is that
once you learn to hold your breath underwater
you'll realise it feels natural

Lungs should burn like an unholy corrosion
Like a negroni you buy just to relax your mouth a little

At least no one makes small talk when they're swimming

                or treads a conversation around and around and around
the kitchen of your friend's friend's house party

Pity that if you yell at the sky it sounds like disturbance
but scream under currents and it's laughter bubbled into
pearled pops and gargled sound bites

Without any of the

- What do you mean by that
- Lol IDGI
- So how do you know the host?

        texts afterwards

        Talking is like swallowing iron pills
        I would public protest with black tape, bound wrists and
            a righteous
        vow of silence just to avoid it

A peak hour Kmart line of salmon dancing
A panting fish jogging up the street, clutching its pedometer
A huge blue squid redirecting its oceanic migration route
to avoid bumping into someone they knew

(Ariel knew)

I can hold my breath for about 30 seconds
which bizarrely is the same amount of time
I can keep up a phone conversation

Remuera

we knew it was over when we saw the borders of our fingers blur rapid against creased thighs when our faces ran out of boundaries borders marred by endless meetings artifice and orifice double death eaters sucking the light out of each other forgetting to draw healthy curtains once the switch became a friction licking earwax from erogenous caverns we let you enter us in public space are broken to stronghold you love us with gentler arms brown doors and wet fingers sex is a skin graft but a whimpered finality becomes a repeat ending split ends as common as archived inconsequence in the arched back of morning we break we line dash we promise we get better we will stop fingering our absences we will not fail our learners we will get a car like an adult and sunset our issues to implosion fast enough to put our woes straight on DVD release we want you to fuck us separate instead of whole again we sit miles apart and make civil conversation meet in a cafe and play out fights like filmic mosquito bites we exchange the names of lovers like worn business cards our snakes for hands inch up a ladder of common sense we are a dog in competition a bitch in heat and in order to necromance fidelity we say the obvious thing like please give us back our inability we are an island of scrutiny a swing bridge of colonies and *no thanks I'll pay for my own coffee*

dumplings are fake

i'm so authentic i use chopsticks to eat macaroni
watch hentai on my huawei
and go to ponsonby central to eat chinese

i don't carry hot sauce in my bag, but i do bring soy to the party
my favourite movie of all time is *studio ghibli*
and my dad is the white side of the family

every time auckland council says 'diversity targets', my phone vibrates
i get suggested ads for the national party in chinese
and that think piece on bubble tea is a redirect to my
dot com slash about me

my mum she love the white man at her dinner table
he tell me to say something in my language
so i say 'hello'
and he say wow! say something else!

so authentic that when i hugged my granddad on my trip home
he froze at the shock of intimacy
because . . . we are that great at building walls

my great-grandma would walk up and down a mountain
with bound feet and huge sacks of rice on her back
for her husband, and i can't even text a guy back

guilt is an after-school curricular
filial piety an apology

my best representation is in a section of pornhub
where all the skinny asian girls and the mixed chicks don't speak
have big tits, and white men cum all over their faces

i posted about it on snapchat the other day
then a dude screenshotted my next selfie

so authentic i was already just a space that needed filling
something to discipline
tall poppy in a sea of lotus,
                              blooming

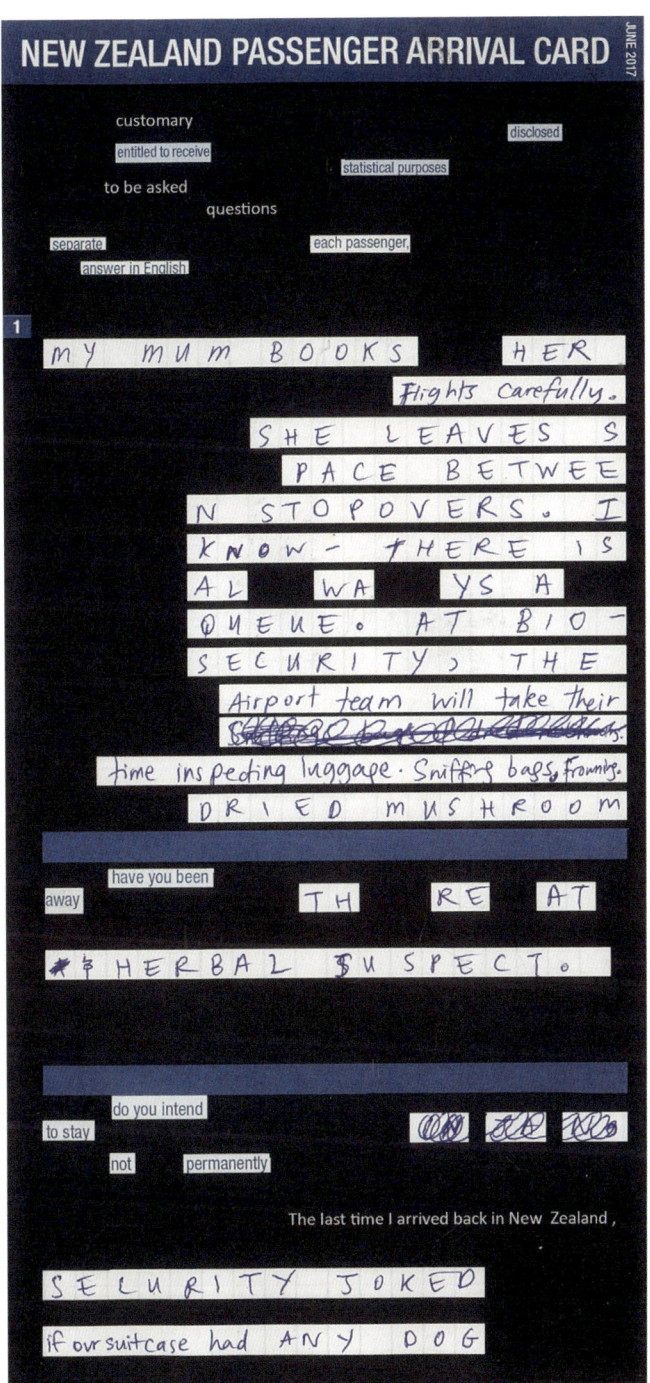

ptsd memes for the anxious / avoidant teen

At least three men have told me I'm the best sex they've ever had but that must be a lie because I'm almost always dissociating. I must be the world's best clown and the world's worst porn actress.	I feel like they must know that I'm faking it because I'm so stiff and unfriendly like a vodka shot. This is not a sexy drink, it is a practical means of dissolving reality.
so I say some shit like *yeah, i love it so much* and continue feeling my hands disappear underneath me.	Maybe it's Maybelline or maybe we're all just living in the matrix. On WhatsApp my sister tells me how she keeps derealising when she's driving her scooter on the motorway.

It makes me concerned for their own moral accountability that they're so into the fact that I'm so obviously failing to appear into them and are not actually invested in the moment we are sharing.	They ask me if I like it or what I'm thinking about. I've been trying to keep up with where we are up to on *Lara Croft: Tomb Raider* 'cause we are 15 minutes in and she just got busted at the temple trying to avenge her father's weird time clock,
Dissociating at the gym when the exercise gets too physical. Dropping a plate while washing the dishes and it sounds like someone raising his voice.	Loud noises feel like white college boys from high school debating telling you you're not only wrong but stupid.

Call me beautiful I won't believe you, free space. Intimacy will kill me, free space.	How many men are hosting unprotected safe spaces w/ vulnerable young women and people of colour and not thinking about the ramifications of their own power?
I've worked really hard catfishing the internet, you would think people would appreciate the effort of me working hard to look hot and unattainable online.	When I was around my family in Malaysia I realised that all the features I hated about my body were almost all the parts of me that connected me back to being Chinese.

Not just dead people have out-of-body experiences.	Staring at my face and wondering when I will start to resemble someone I could point out in a crowd and say, *she looks nice* about. It's kind of rude that everyone can just see me at all angles.
It's painful to realise that the people around you know more about what you look like than you do yourself. The temperature of social cues.	What is really painful is wanting so badly to touch someone and then feeling repulsed by that same instinct.

There's Real Mānuka Honey in Heaven

in the year 3000,
lizards will be the last survivors of remaining world order
but it doesn't matter because we're all going to die!

in twenty-two years I'll be hitting my midlife crises
as the Amazon finally collapses from heartburn
a wizened crone releasing the IV drip from glazed root veins

a global conference of bees will be livestreamed strapping on
army helmets khaki stripes and matching jetpacks
then flying off into the stratosphere in tiny astronautical booties

the bonnets left behind had their URGENT: agenda emails
marked as spam but who cares about Spam
when we'll live underwater and eat raw salmon everyday
and if we're poisoned then we'll relocate

leaving the planet, it's one small step for man!
as all the mammals left on Earth's Ark
study home & garden magazines as textual predecessors
that foreshadow our ecological demise
under the watchful eyes of agricultural industries

while the tuatara sings a eulogy to the end of the Anthropocene

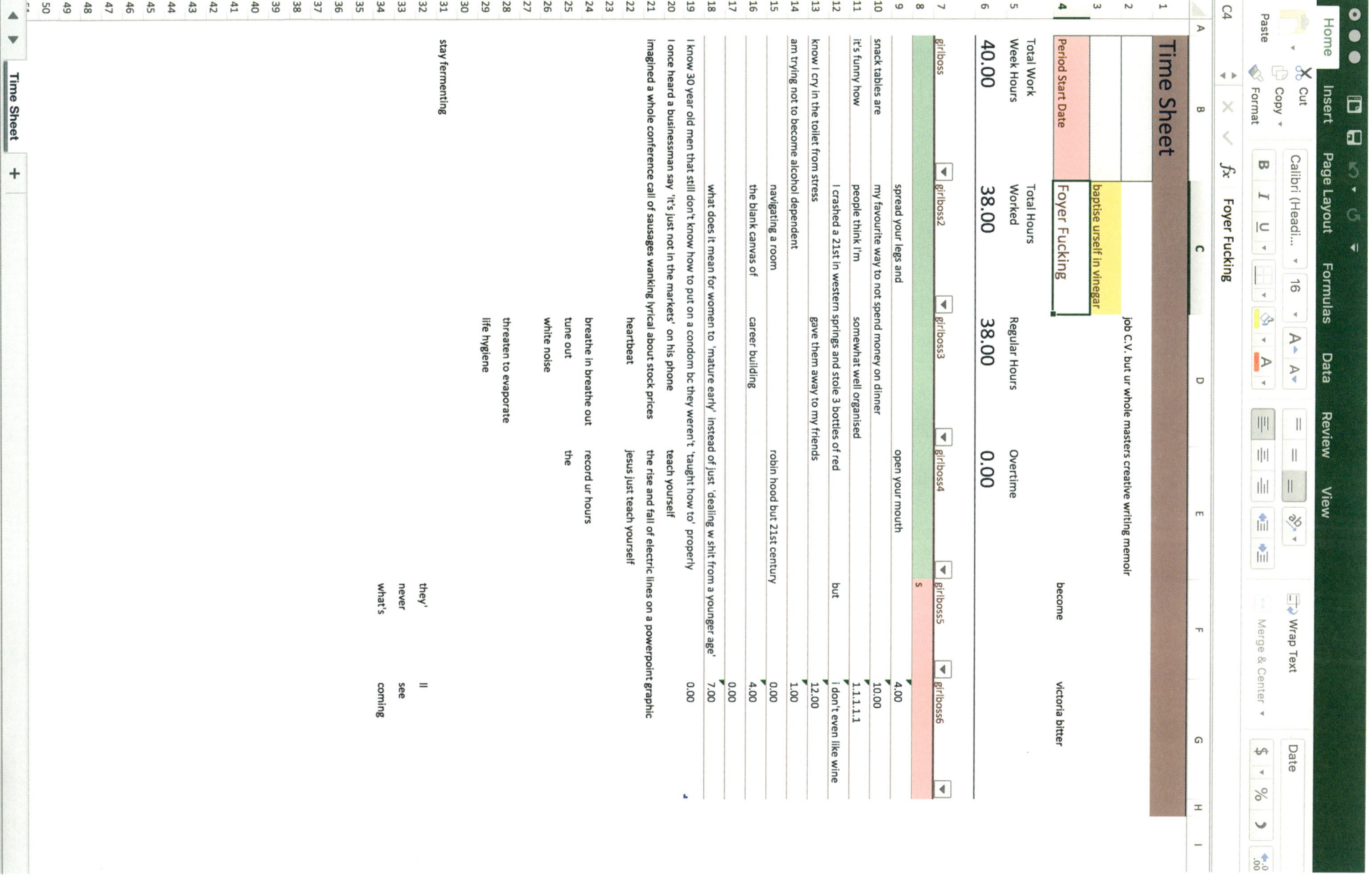

beauty

beauty was a stone in your pocket, an advantage, a summer heat thrown downriver, your unrequited crush, mosquitoes in unrelenting torrents, fake tan on slim ankles, the circumference of a pearl, a rage that rang inside your ears and sharpened thoughts to splinters

beauty was a stone ███████ advantage a ███ heat thrown downriver, your ██████████████ mosquito nets in ███████ fake tan ███ the circumference of ██████ a rage that rang inside your ears and made you want to shatter

███ was a stone advantage, a thrown heat, a rush to reassemble hairpins ███ the crease of your voice ████████████████ when he told you about his online searches ████ stalking iron on cellulite ███ ██████████ something to dismiss and then ritualise ██████████ █████████ █████ ████████ a circumstantial laughter

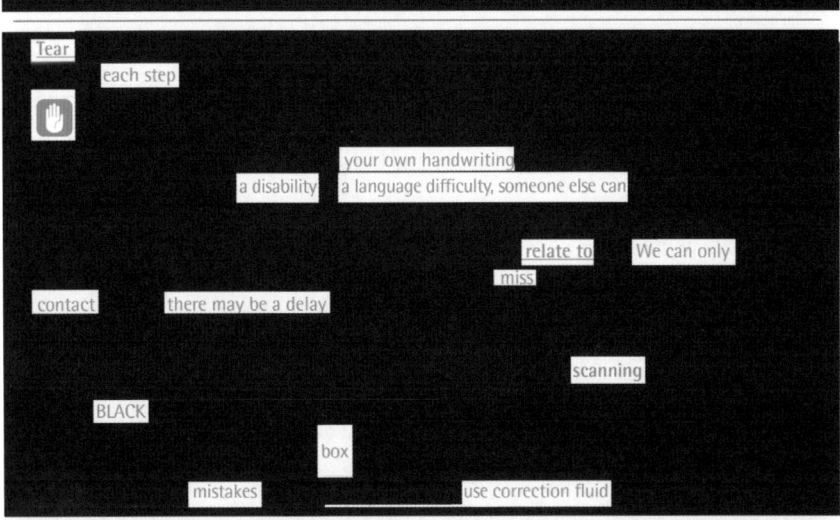

Tear
each step
your own handwriting
a disability   a language difficulty, someone else can
relate to   We can only
miss
contact   there may be a delay
scanning
BLACK
box
mistakes   use correction fluid

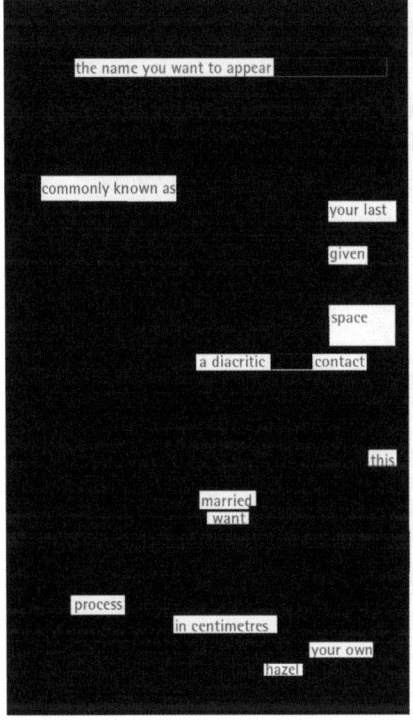

the name you want to appear

commonly known as
your last
given
space
a diacritic   contact

this
married
want

process
in centimetres
your own
hazel

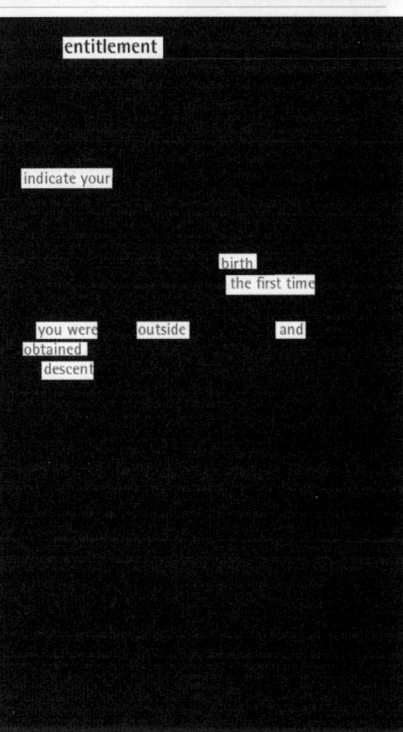

entitlement

indicate your

birth
the first time
you were   outside   and
obtained
descent

Recipe for a Funeral

★★★★☆

Cook time: 60 minutes | Easy | Serves: 30–100

Impress your guests with this bittersweet chocolate cherry gateau, a revamped version of a retro classic. Bound to delight, considering you have no retirement funds.

Ingredients:

- The top three award-winning butter sculptures from Iowa State Fair
- Every block of chocolate that Whittaker's can produce on a night shift
- Your bodyweight in the morning, measured in flour
- One bathtub of caster sugar, marinated by dusk
- A full head of hair's worth of cocoa
- As many eggs as you can steal from a free-range farm
- One shaken pump bottle filled with bicarbonate of soda
- More buttercream than can be weighed on a bathroom scale
- A bag of refrigerated O+ donated blood
- One Himalayan salt lamp with working batteries, left to thaw

To assemble:

- All the cherries you can cram in your mouth, stolen from a South Island fruit farm
- A jar of strawberry jam, untouched in purgatory
- The topmost layer of a nebulous cloud
- Four pack of Smirnoff Ice from the kitchen bench of a teen house party
- A retirement village's rose garden, dipped in sugar
- Countdown's supply of Chewy Caramel Tim Tams
- One pack freeze-dried raspberry powder
- One pack Nestlé choc bits
- Store-bought fondant

Method:

1. Rent crematorium the morning of or day prior to the funeral. Heat cremator to 180°C. Grease and line casket (180 × 55 cm). Boil the kettle. Melt butter sculptures and chocolate in transfer pan. Gently heat until melted.
2. Crush Himalayan salt lamp in an industrial food processor. Place with other dry ingredients in an XL-sized urn loader. Add pinch of soil. Sift.
3. Scrape wet mixtures into urn loader, add boiling water and whizz by throwing on an electric fence until the batter is lump free.
4. Call your mother while stirring gently.
5. Pour mixture into caskets and bake for 25 minutes in cremator.
6. Prick with the anxiety of whether you're getting into heaven. Allow thoughts to cool to room temperature. Carefully cut body-sized trench into middle layer of cake using large dessert spoon. Place the pillowy body of a loved one in the middle of the batter. Keep body cryogenically frozen until time of baking.
7. Mix together Smirnoff Ice, juiced cherries and bag of donated blood. Drizzle over the cake, letting the earthy flavours mingle with the cocoa into a complex mélange of grief and stunning beauty.
8. Tip half of a nebulous cloud into a separate transfer pan and heat until just below evaporation. Chop chocolate, then slowly add in until the texture resembles clotted cream.
9. Stack cakes, with body placed firmly in the middle layer and pinned in place with clothes pegs. Dollop jam and sky between layers. Decorate surface with buttercream, sugared roses, freeze-dried raspberry powder and Nestlé choc bits. Place wafer-thin white chocolate with *Sorry for your loss* message in centre (this sign can be purchased in advance from a local baker). Pipe small rows of fondant across the periphery like dewy morning grass. Layer a row of Tim Tams along the bottom like gravestones. Pile remaining fresh cherries in and around the cake. Serve immediately.
10. Bon Appétit!

Comments, Questions and Tips:

MirandaJuly
★★★★☆
Delicious! I made a smaller version of this for the death of my cat. Just third the mixture.

KayFee
★★★★★
Wow, this is a gorgeous recipe. Made this for my Uncle's funeral and got high praise for it. Lovely and moist. Like a cordon bleu except as a dessert. One tip I picked up … I put in extra party poppers and popcorn with the body. The children got such a fright when Brian's hungry, ghostly resurrected corpse turned up and had enough spiritual laissez-faire to burst out of the cake during the mourning procession. It was a delightful stripper-cake-cum-casket but make sure the younger ones have napkins and diapers ready!

mykitchendrools
★★☆☆☆
Got served this 'pièce de résistance' at my grandmother's funeral. Thank God there was yoghurt served with it because it was so dry I almost bit into her arm just to get a bit of moisture. Make sure to bake for less time than the recipe suggests.

(🤐)

Didn't you try to 💋 the boy's full lip
a smiling crescent
When all you knew of open mouths
were men at 🎉 forcing their 👅 down.

Weren't you an open 🥪 for the restless
didn't you deserve it
didn't you want to be 😵 😵 😵
in private

a 🤚 cupping soil in the garden
didn't you glamorise the empty rooms
the open 🏗️ but *just imagine when the light hits*

When your wrists plunge and pucker
like creases in the couch fabric

Didn't you try to excuse their 🔥
for the way they dug in
didn't you call it *gardening*,
call it *maintenance* with a stronger grip

Didn't you try to 🚫 🍆
didn't you try to 🗣️
didn't you laugh 🔊
until the 😂 😂 😂
started leaking through the plastic

SHOPPING LIST
OF SMALL VIOLENCES.

- GRINDING YOUR TEETH AT NIGHT
- PICKING YOUR LIPS UNTIL THE SKIN PEELS OFF
- POPPING PIMPLES UNTIL THEY SCAR
- UNDERWEAR
- DRINKING SO MUCH YOU THROW UP IN A POT PLANT
- TYING YOUR HAIR UP
- NOT CUTTING YOUR NAILS

- THE FORK SCRAPE OF TOOTH ON METAL
- BEROCCA PERFORMANCE
- GLUTEN FREE UP'N' GOS
- WAITING ON SOMEONE'S TEXT RESPONSE TO FULFIL YOUR IMMEDIATE NEED FOR INTIMACY
- OVERLY TIGHT JEANS
- FROZEN MEALS
- A TATTOO OF AN INFINITY SYMBOL
- TOUCHING THE KETTLE TO SEE IF IT'S HOT
- COVERING YOUR SCARS WITH CONCEALER
- LOOKING AT THE TIME TOO MUCH

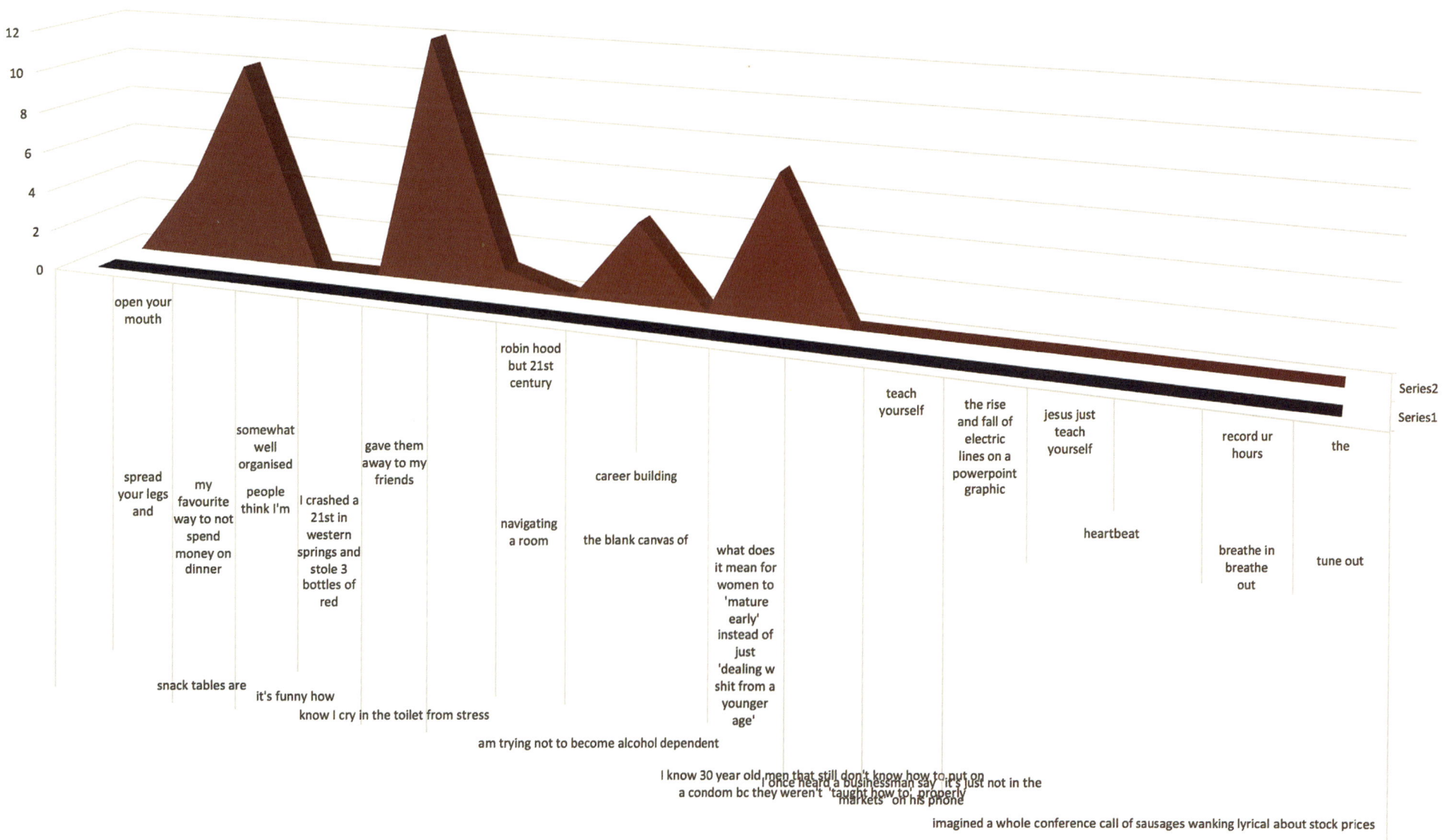

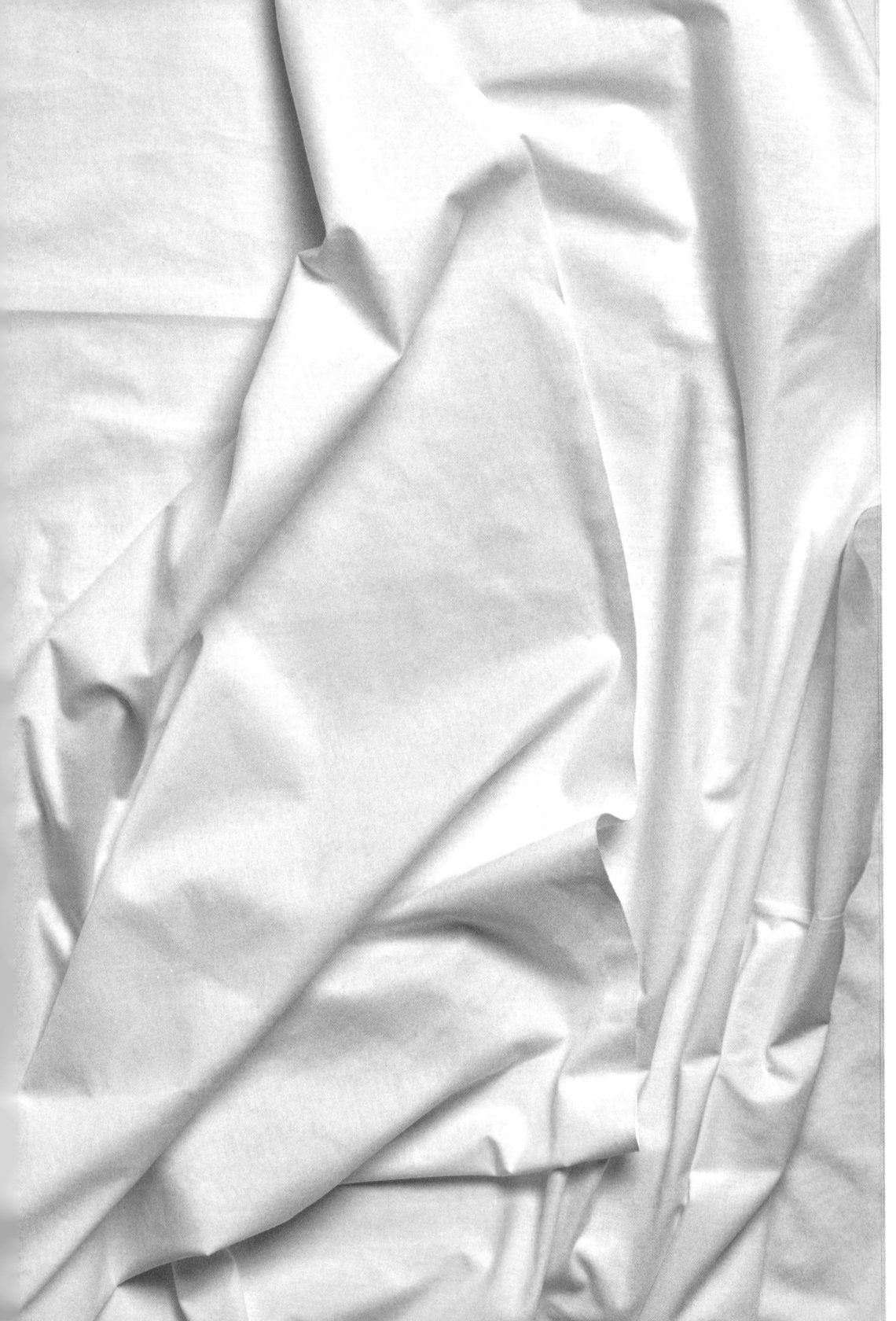

Glory Be to Family Planning

Patron saint of pill poppers
holy house of halfway decisions
home of the cream
the rash
the cranberry intrauterine

Glory to how we drop in late and pyjama shuffle
our excuses to stern-faced nurses
with lab coats for wings

Unused condoms
roaming a hungry wasteland of sheets

In the background
Brad and Angelina are still together
the radio crinkles stripped-back décor
and tabloids from our parents' era

I've never been so proud to fail a test
pamphlets still tucked into the lining of my uterus

But the crow's feet shift and fidget
from queues and absences
and careless, careless pledges

Hell hath no fury like
your whole body gambled
in front of the receptionist

Hopeless missed stakes
dry lacunal ellipses

Raise your legs to Family Planning
those red prescriptive questions
that satan of a speculum

Glory most of all to the nurse who receives me
as I run straight through those glass doors

The first person to take my pressure
uncrumple my body

Watch me consume pauses
like glasses of water

Then ask if I love him
Then ask if I'm sure

EX-PARTNERS
HAVE CALLED
ME A BAPTISM,

I CALLED THEM
A HEADACHE

I want to know every
element of how you were
hurt so I can form a
rugby game strategy

Love, like rugby,
I just don't understand
It looks like interpetive
dance to me
Like a ~~too~~ crowd for the
Hurricanes screaming wildly
into their vuvuzelas

"YOU ARE
CARED FOR
AND VALUED
INHERENTLY"

two-piece bathing suits

i.

I was never the girl brave enough to undress in public changing rooms.

Some girls, like Annabel, would get straight to it, whipping their tops off like they were born naked or something. They shimmied their limbs into sparkly two-piece bikinis while still managing to convey with hushed delivery how Harry had confessed to Emma after school yesterday up the tree at Ben Burn park. *But what did she say?* We whispered through the changing room turned auditorium.

When I was a gangly, nine-year-old amphibian, I loved to be in the water. I had weekly lessons and regularly ran from our car door all the way to the waves. Swimming pools only became terrifying once I noticed the public audience to my limbs, that the boys in your class could see you for what you were: naked and ashamed under chlorinated spandex.

Plastic bands wrung our hair out like flannels as we wobbled a wet line between child and adult, wisps of adolescence jutting out of nylon underwear.

ii.

Before one of our regular swimming lessons, Annabel turned to me and Cathy as we were juggling between togs undies togs undies togs public decency and whispered:

Did you know I heard from Sarah who saw Cathy getting dressed by accident that Cathy has hair down there?

By *there*, she meant pubic region, the scariest neighbourhood a girl could live. Annabel was waiting for me to react so I gasped half-heartedly, because she scared the shit out of me and I didn't want to be the weird kid.

Cathy was the weird kid. Her family had wacko problems like mine and everyone thought she was secretly a lesbian. Fearing the worst, I mumbled *real strange* and backed into a private changing room, Annabel's eyes piercing through the wood. I hunched into a plain black bathing suit that hid as much of myself as possible and made sure not to look at anyone's bodies while I exited.

iii.

The first time I remember feeling the divide between what I looked like and what I might grow into was sharing the shower with my mum. She had river lines across her stomach. I was soft toddler limbs and pink puppy fat. God did not answer my pleas to stop growing, so I turned pliant under hormonal tweezers. My limbs swelled in response to B cups fondled under the pretence of watching movies. My thighs thickened to trunks. I filled out and grew higher, bigger, similar still. I took my baths fully clothed, my body a wrong no amount of soap could erase. And then I swam naked.

iv.

We were born into buoyancy. Our births were the first great waterpark features. We were born into cellulite publicity, each wrinkle practised a thousand times over. Before I move, I practise how I might be seen, scrutinise the pores of my laughter. Goggles are my only defence each time I try and swim through public space.

v.

Sunday evenings are my routine swim days. I walk to Tepid Baths as the sun casts its showcase and leave by day's ovation. The way I reclaim muscle memory is to swim faster than attention, up and down the lanes. When I am in the water, I am nothing but a concerted effort to keep moving. I wade through the swim caps and bobbing lanes, heavy enough to sink, and save myself from drowning.

+ / −

I don't have a heater that's operational at the moment but I do have blankets to shield from porous housing and if I don't have enough resource to survive an apocalypse then I do have the beauty of hindsight in a rear-view mirror so I didn't eat breakfast this morning because I couldn't use the toaster but I did have enough money to buy a feed and friends who would shout me if I told them I was hungry and yes I don't have time anymore but I do have a job and that means regular wages and if I don't have a job or I quit then I do have an art practice, a parent to the rescue, a slightly less shitty government and a half-wrung CV so I don't have money but I don't have an overdraft either I don't have money because I do have money enough to not have money as I have the ability to spend in mild decadence on books and clothes and dinners and causes I believe in and I don't have a four-poster bed but I do have clean sheets, fabric softener and dirty chandeliers I don't have a clean bedroom but I do have a vacuum if and when I want to use that I don't have time but I can share my Google calendar moments stolen from schedules like breaking off a piece of bread to bump into someone and cowboy boogie if I don't have the coordination to dance very technically then at least I have free uninhibited reign over my body and I do have two legs and I do know how to move them and my body for the most part obeys me if it has been aching then that's always been for a reason and if I'm hungry then I do think to myself to eat and if I'm in pain then I am at least in conversation on the days I don't like myself I do have other people and on the days I don't like other people I do have *My Own Private Idaho* film references to insert and books to gloat over on Goodreads so if I don't have electricity then at least I have a working shower that blasts from hot to cold so fast the steam fogs up my memory and if I don't have wifi then I do have a cell phone to ask my mother how cold it is in another city and if I feel trapped then I do have the ability to leave no one will hurt me if I disagree on the worst days when I don't have anything except an empty fridge of functioning then I do have friends who pull me out of my misery sheets to watch *Ferris Bueller's Day Off* from a hospital bed and when I have rocks in pocket bottoms then I must have a coat to put them in or someone that put that on me so I do have a body and I do know how to use it and if I don't have deficiencies then I must have a surplus.

The Capital of My Mother

My mother was born in the capital of Malaysia
her own umbilical cord tied to a deflating sun

In her country, the heat is wet
the air is heady
the sweat on my back is hereditary

I know no kin except blood tied to bone
my water body leaks red and diaspora yellow
these eyes are globes

Karl, my brother, is turning seven
We sit in the muggy backyard of our grandparents' house

Kuala Lumpur means muddy confluence
The city is born from the place two rivers
merge then flow

I am the point two paths cross just to separate
by-product of my parents' relations
divorce impeding
my mother's birthplace

They say all rivers flow to sea
I cannot find home except the sense
of somewhere I can't reach
I am a migrant's remembrance
I am a welcome party

The kettle is boiling and it is time in slow motion
It is the noise of my grandma learning English
off my five-year-old cousin

Her R's are a dysfunctional lawnmower
explaining *wet season*, *sticky rice*, *tang yuan*

Across the phone
in my privileged NZ accent
I talk about burgers, flat whites, fries with aioli

We don't speak the same language
but we do share the same ocean
when I say noodles she knows exactly what I mean

Potluck is God doing dishes
Migration is the earth stirring flavour
Clepsydra is a clock that runs from dripping liquid
Its name means water thief

Across boats, migrants tell time by the second
and we call them thieves for different reasons

But the first house I live in is a transported container
stolen body, claimed land, white heartbeat

Decades are tides that rock us to sleep
except landlocked I cannot dream
except I have a fear of the open sea
accept that you are dry land
still amniotic
barren
bleeding

I've worn ships not shoes since the minute
I was aware of my own unbound feet

Only a daughter's daughter's body
arriving to this space every century

The harbour is a welcome mat
for a new placenta

I spit in it
and let the land claim my whole front teeth

To All the Boys I've Loved Before

A drove his Mercedes quiet
like the sigh of steamed bao
but wove his hands too close so
I swung that block button like Chun Li

>*R* told me he missed me
>jacking off to black hair clouding
>neon screens

F had a new half-Asian babe
to replace his old half-Asian ex
but I was his current screenshot

>*T* told me my eyes were lovely

J was Korean but
hated himself deeply

>*M* loved redheads and kawaii
>… so lucky I am a mixed-breed Ferrari

F surfed asianbabes.net but
I've always preferred swimming

I suspected *S* of a fetish once 'cause they
banged an exchange student

>I suspected *J* 'cause he liked miniature figurines

For *X* I pressed my B cups into A-grade décolletage
and informed him that his kinks were just lightly fermented misogyny

>*B* heard I strode around
>in latex skirts, strumming on my abacus

C's mum put me in the annual Christmas newsletter
She'd heard I lost weight and spoke good English

                                        Z loved my pussy for the slant of its eyeliner
                               the slop of pungent crushed garlic fermenting in my undies

Y heard I could make a dragon
roar like a waterfall
just at the sight of a thigh slit

                                                            I came from
                                                          down the road

                                                  guess my whatever
                                                like a genre of music

my skin white like ... rice porridge

my
city of ethnics
unravelled
like a strip tease

Chris
Stewart

Gravity

navigator

I remember the first bearing of love
our backs on the midnight grass
the summer air stopped warm
as fingers charted skin

we lay inside the moon's road
saw directions to the future
I pulled a star down
from the map of the sky
drew a plot of it in my voice for you
I crawled inside that message
nestled through the calm of your hair
and waited to be opened

now your thoughts lie in the earth's still latitude
dissipated like the archaeology of stardust
I return from the sky
to navigate the cartography of us

gravity

before I clamp
and cut a length of time grown
from the black hole of your belly
the midwife interprets placenta
the way astronomers read constellations
a loop in the cord the myth of your departure
I hear nostalgia for the womb
the way light misses the hearts of stars
we glove the light in our skin
find sleep in solar wind
wrap ourselves in the gravity
of your arrival

everyone wants to know how heavy they are

you bear them to the scales
not because they're heavy; it's the weight
of the thought you might lose
balance and trip
they look cold on that weighing dish
after that you try not to measure them
there are proper ways to lift them when
they grow into dumbbells
one day you notice new muscles in your back
then you can hardly pick them up
when everyone wants to know how heavy they are
what weighs on you isn't knowing the kilograms
but the force
with which you are pulled towards them

embers

the first time we bathed
our daughter in the lounge
it was dark except for the fireplace
she lay between us and flickered
the chiaroscuro was so solid
in the water it etched
still frames in our memory
some say humans evolved staring
into waves of fire
sheltered precious embers from rain
settled the arctic with flame
and old religions of the sun
we painted shadows when we dried her
modelled light around her curves
you said you saw the stroke of another
crease on my face
perhaps my forehead stretch-marked
as my frontal lobe grew
a new fold

flecks of ice

on the day your life ends everyone else
who matters is born
you dig deep
holes to put decades to sleep
you expect to grow wings
instead you hear clocks
all you do is watch
little hands pass through bars into new spaces
on the day you feel surrounded
by dirt you look out of the grave to see
angels wear half-blended faces of your ancestors
this type of death is thinking
you are above it all
but you are below
this type of death is waking up
every sleep cycle to feel
your beard has grown
new flecks of ice

mummy

midnight opens
with your eyes I travel
my Nile to rub your teeth
shamble with my arms
in front of me sometimes
I want to leave you
without these bandages
this wrap of weight my own
will bottled in a spiked interior
they say the iron maiden was
the shape of a sarcophagus
I cannot lean on any side
until you sleep

you have too many dreams to be asleep

after you wake three times
three hundred and sixty-five times
you cannot close
your eyes at home
any man who finds
work at home finds home at work
you cannot close your eyes at work
sick of work
you cannot call in sick from home
in a year of sleep you never complete
a dream

a tooth emerges

after milk teeth cut
nights to pieces the memory

of a tooth below gums is
an incomplete dream

they used to think teething
was a cause of death

in their sympathetic magic
strong bones were teething toys

now I am a sore tooth pulled
from a soft bed

my swollen nerves erupt
you only see my crown

but my roots are still
embedded in the bone

you take a tunnel to the sea

at midnight the hallway
is a channel through rock
to a cave that might be
your universe if it were not
for a lack of stars
as you rock a daughter in
the womb of a mountain
you just want to lick
the ocean's arms open
but you are too far
from the mouth to see
the white eye
you just hear the hurtle
of a headlight haunt
towards you like
a drip
of water ripples
to a grinding
wave

time's handle locks from the inside

in a family of walls locked
doors hold their bones in confidence

doors never see what hides
behind their backs

secrets pass loud-mouthed
doors like light through glass

a door can be a hole in the ice
the penguin as it rises sees

a leopard seal
wait in a seam of light

confidence in doors can be
a hole in the ground

unless held ajar at night
to let in a little light

children's doors might
as well be walls

I have no juice for you to suck

a baby waking at night is
a lick of lemon
and the nights of lemon season last
all year under drowsy slices of moon
they tell me I should never let
your dimpled face that glows
in the dark fall asleep on me
easy for them to say when every time
sleep sprouts the wind
taps lemons on your window to unpeel
our sour faces
lemons are the only fruit
in the world with a negative charge
the lemon seed of your sleep is so
small the wax of my skin yellows
they say a lemon tree can live
a hundred years
in the morning I'll chop
the whole thing down

profit

in granite wombs pressure forms
veins of gold
we mine for mother lodes
shovel pans for days only
to discover value
in digging
children are either nuggets or
the mine

there are no angels but the children of mice and eagles

I know worms who swaddle
babies in silk the way a penguin
sits on his egg until it hatches, waiting
for his wife to bring fish
every scorpion is wary of his daughter's sting
I saw an eagle watch her chicks stab each other
turtles tell me to hide my children in shells
I went to the panda she told me
to leave one daughter behind
I went to the mouse he told me
to eat both my daughters
I went to the worm it told me
to let my daughters eat me
if I was a polar bear I would wrap
my children in a burrow of snow
being a horse I just buckle
my saddle to my back

male seahorses bear the young

in another life I had no stomach yet I grew
fifty eggs in a pouch of belly skin before I released
flurries of fully formed miniature seahorses
in another life I died of exhaustion
a terrible swimmer caught
in a storm-roiled sea with only
small fins to steer myself
bigger fish told me when you have children
your life is over
some say at the end you hear the sea
I hear the sea is the best place to be born
if you have fins on your spine that flutter

scarf

before bed we wrap
lengths of our day around us
we notice as we grow we choose
stories with fewer pictures
today I told Audrey to wear
her jacket or she'd turn into a snowman
now I say I knew a man with
sticks for arms who wore a top hat
when he sat too close to the fire
his spine melted
what we know about sleep is
we can't dress ourselves
after we switch the lights off
it's dark
at the end of the day
we only have this scarf

rusty bones

in the Neolithic age you couldn't help
a childhood full of monsters

to avoid man-eating megafauna
you fossilised yourself

these days monsters hardly eat children
although the roadside still petrifies us

at the museum we discover the world's first traffic accident
once this two-year-old ran straight out of the cave

horns through millennia hit me
like a monolith falls

her rusty bones are frozen here
in the headlights of a sabre-toothed tiger

inflammation

in the respiratory room the nebuliser
hisses its mist in spits

bees speak the language of your lungs
your chest tightens its hives

nurses buzz off without saying
how long they leave us

down corridors skinny as
your trachea becomes

the passage of air through lungs is alchemy
oxygen opens into blood the way

fingers filter hair
bronchi divide into branches small

as the idea of breath
if my breath was Ventolin

I would tunnel through the comb
of your wax to kill bees

to loosen the sting
of honey on your lungs

in the respiratory room songs of bees
enflame organs in chests other than lungs

Russian dolls

the health of babies depends on
the health of grandmothers

your mother was born with your eggs
your grandmother grew them inside her

your great-grandmother sculpted
porcelain dolls with heads

the shape of my mother's
never painted or polished

they remained white as hard
boiled eggs

today you will only eat eggs
what passes your mouth is

only hard boiled
only white

your grandmother on your mother's side
fed your mother what was inside her

she kept chickens
eggs they laid had brittle shells

but they had grit
but they had whites like steak

they were the best eggs
you've ever eaten

your father was also buried

your father was made
of the air it took

to breathe for your
suffocated mother

when she was left
with holes your father

filled them with earth
even with earth

some holes couldn't be filled
then your father was made

of the wind it took
to blow the earth off

your buried mother
in the ice he found water

to sooth her burns
then your father was

the fire it took
to warm her

frost

to see if baking was done
my mother taught me to stick the knife in
she took the cake sunken

from the oven to show me
how to ice it over
my father was a cake she baked

once she arrived home caked
in too much make-up and perfume
as she withdrew

the knife from her excuse I saw
a mixture still tacky to the blade
when I bake now I also think

of Chocolate our cat
she said ran away
I never told her I uncovered

his bones one winter by mistake
poking through patches of broken
earth decorated by patterns of ice

this morning as we lower her
I remember the way
she covered herself

I notice thin layers
of frost protect
the dirt

my father the elephant

I have a grey memory
of my father the elephant
his ears brushed the dust
on my mother but I never
heard his trumpet fountain
any water when her skin was dry
sometimes he arrived home late
to walk on the tips of his fingers
Mum made him sleep standing up
I remember the night I heard
the mud in his wallow
at the height of drought her nails
worn to the sponge my mother
decided to charge she tucked
her ears against her neck
folded her trunk under
her chin before she swayed
backwards and forwards
surprisingly silent and
trampled the final door
later that night I crept
up the tips of his fingers
into the water of his purr
the last time I saw him
his trunk was raised
like a snorkel

The history of his bridge

We remember the flood. He shadowed us
rain-soaked children in the doorway.

The broken paddle in his hands
the mustard seed of joblessness.

When he turned, we watched time churn
through our awestruck seconds,

heard the touch of wind
but could not know the distance it blew,

saw puddles under his feet but not
the sound of gumboots clap steps.

Years later, torrents dam into soft rivers.
We all paddle the trickle of time.

Branches sprawl strong enough
from his mustard trunk to settle birds.

In the rain, his footmarks
gather no water.

the chef

peeling carrots he hears
the winter voice of his mother's recipe
stew cheap cuts of meat
remembers the red taste of it
blown on a wooden spoon remembers
the braise was cooked with ash remembers
the day his mother chopped her finger like a carrot
at the compost heap he measures
the weight of onion skins
with the moisture in his eyes
the memory of his mother
a smoking hāngī

Like stone flowers a dead man

Because you don't know
what to mean or how to sound,
your sound has no meaning.
Because your cool has no sound, no meaning
can cool your sound. Dreadlocks watch
you furious and still as rocks morph
into girls whose sharp-toothed eyes bite
into your heart of snow. At dance parties
you bite back with the teeth of your heart.
Words lounge into lines. When it's over,
you frame your mind on the wall.

For years of work the alcohol of sleep blocks
the fledged noise of you. You grow out
of high school hang-ups like regrowth in high school hair.
Infinite potential collapses into one path.
They say experience learns a boy into different men.
You say the experience of difference buds
the teeth of men into soft pearls.
The difference is always a woman.

You fix her in your eyes and see her.
You suck her into your belly and breathe her.
You call her with the marrow of your lungs.
You cup her to your ear and hear her.
You carry her in the voice of your arms.
You love her with the shiver of your skin.
You marry her with the ring of your finger.

Now you rock
your children like porcelain dolls cradled on your chest.
You can't lift a grain of stolen time.
You hear autumn breezes scrape
dry leaves over concrete paths, listen
for the sparrow, wait

for the summer seagull to swoop overhead.
The clicks of insects are the switches of lights
and the veins of winter bloom across your forehead
like stone flowers a dead man.

Notes

The Monks Who Tend the Garden with Tiny Scissors
'Juni-Gatsu' was first recited on Radio New Zealand in an interview
    with Kim Hill
'Food to Song' first appeared in *Best New Zealand Poems*
'Opoutere' first appeared in *Poetry Sz*
'The Essence of I' first appeared in *Blackmail Press*

Shopping List of Small Violences
'Remuera', 'There's Real Mānuka Honey in Heaven' and 'beauty' first
    appeared in *Starling*
'dumplings are fake' first appeared in *Scum Magazine*
'New Zealand Passenger Arrival Card' and 'Guide Notes' first appeared
    in *Hainamana*
'ptsd memes for the anxious / avoidant teen' first appeared in *Mimicry*
'Foyer Fucking' and 'Chart Title' first appeared as part of *AUT Art and
    Design Festival* at St Paul St Gallery
'Shopping List of Small Violences' first appeared in *The Mood Machine*
    by Satellites
'two-piece bathing suits' first appeared in *Turbine | Kapohau*
'The Capital of My Mother' first appeared in *Poetry Shelf*
'To All the Boys I've Loved Before' first appeared in *Sport*

Gravity
'navigator' first appeared in *Snorkel*
'gravity' and 'mummy' first appeared in *Sweet Mammalian*
'my father the elephant' first appeared in *Brief*
'The history of his bridge' first appeared in *takahē*
'your father was also buried' first appeared in *Landfall*

Ben Kemp works as a primary school teacher in Papua New Guinea where he has lived for the past three years with his diplomat wife and three children. Gisborne-born Kemp arrived in the Pacific following six years in Australia and ten years in Japan. Tokyo was where he discovered his passion for Kabuki theatre and Japanese film and literature. Between 2003 and 2010 he recorded three studio albums with his band Uminari and toured in Japan, Australia and New Zealand. His artistic work has often explored the nexus between Japanese and Māori/Polynesian culture. He credits the late Taupō-based Māori writer and mentor Rowley Habib with helping him tap into poetry and original writing in his twenties.

Vanessa Crofskey (born in 1996) is a writer and artist of Hokkien Chinese and Pākehā descent. She graduated from Auckland University of Technology with a degree in sculpture in 2017. Through her practice she investigates social connection: how we form identities through intimacy, inheritance, location and violence. Vanessa has published and presented widely as an interdisciplinary artist – in performance spaces, galleries, festivals plus digital and print publications. She has written for *The Spinoff*, *Gloria Books*, *New Zealand Herald*, *Dear Journal*, *Hainamana* and other serious publishing places. She is also a two-time poetry slam champion and award-winning theatre maker but we promise that doesn't detract from the rest of her career and personality. Vanessa currently works for *The Pantograph Punch* as a staff writer, and as a curator at Window Gallery (University of Auckland). She advocates for complex trauma survivors and those with attention deficit disorder, plus is very funny and knows a lot about what snacks to eat.

Chris Stewart was born in Wellington but grew up in Christchurch. He has a BA in History and Art History with minors in English and education from the University of Otago and two graduate diplomas in teaching. He completed the Hagley Writers' Institute course in 2015, where he won The Margaret Mahy Prize, and his poems have since been published in New Zealand journals such as *Snorkel*, *takahē*, *Sweet Mammalian*, *Brief*, *Catalyst*, *Mimicry*, *Blackmail Press*, *Landfall* and *Aotearotica*. He regularly attends the monthly open mic event 'Catalyst', a forum for literary and performance poets in Christchurch. Most importantly, he is a son, a brother, a husband, and a father.

First published 2020
Auckland University Press
University of Auckland
Private Bag 92019
Auckland 1142
New Zealand
www.press.auckland.ac.nz

© Ben Kemp, Vanessa Crofskey, Chris Stewart, 2020

ISBN 978 1 86940 909 8

Published with the assistance of Creative New Zealand

A catalogue record for this book is available from the National Library of New Zealand

This book is copyright. Apart from fair dealing for the purpose of private study, research, criticism or review, as permitted under the Copyright Act, no part may be reproduced by any process without prior permission of the publisher. The moral rights of the authors have been asserted.

Design by Greg Simpson
Printed in China by Everbest Printing Investment Ltd